Choice Words

A COUPLE'S JOURNAL
TOWARDS BETTER COMMUNICATION

" *Gracious words are like a honeycomb, sweetness to the soul and health to the body*" *Proverbs 16:24*

Choice Words

A COUPLE'S JOURNAL
TOWARDS BETTER COMMUNICATION

" Gracious words are like a honeycomb, sweetness to the soul and health to the body" Proverbs 16:24

Unless otherwise indicated, all Scripture quotations are taken
from the © *Holy Bible, New International Version, NIV,*
King James Version from the Internet at
www.biblegateway.com

CHOICE WORDS:
A COUPLE'S JOURNAL TOWARD BETTER COMMUNICATION

www.gracefullyblended.com
www.delisanewwilliams.com

ISBN: 978-1-09277-726-1
Printed in the United States of America
©2019 by Amielio Williams and DeLisa New Williams

THIS JOURNAL BELONGS TO
MR. AND MRS.

_____

EST.

_____

MAKE IT YOUR GOAL
TO CREATE A

marriage

THAT FEELS LIKE THE
SAFEST PLACE ON
EARTH

Over the years, our marriage has seen it's fair share of ups and downs. During those moments of storms and what looked like despair, when ever one of us tried to tell the other our thoughts or how we felt, it wasn't coming across the way we expected it to for the other person. Words were misconstrued, harsh tones took precedent over words of understanding, and eventually we ended up not communicating to each other at all. Which is exactly what the devil wanted...

But instead of talking face to face to each other because our verbal words were hurting each other more than helping, we would write a letter or email our thoughts. Removing the tone, attitude, and spirit of offense and defense; allowed us to truly "hear" each other's heart.

Therefore, we decided to create a journal for husband and wife, provide some scriptures we've used to believe God for in our marriage, as well as include the very same prayers we've prayed and believed God to heal some areas in our relationship.

Our prayer is this journal will be a tool to bring you two closer as well and create a better foundation for communication in your marriage. We've seen the power of God work in our marriage and through each one of us individually as well as collectively and we believe and agree that he will do the same for you tow.

With love,

Amielio & DeLisa

EXAMPLE JOURNAL ENTRY
A Couple's Words

"Gracious words are like a honeycomb, sweetness to the soul and health to the body" (Proverbs 16:24)

DATE: *March 21, 2019*   TIME: *10:38 p.m.*

THE SITUATION: *For the last couple of days, I've been feeling really neglected by you and I've been trying to tell you, but you haven't listened to me. I had things I needed to accomplish this week which I couldn't do because it seems as your priorities trump mine. And I'm wearing myself thin these last few days. I had so much to handle and you didn't even try to understand or help out at all. Your work schedule is really crazy and I feel like you use that as an excuse to not fulfill my needs and desires. My love language is not being filled and I don't feel intimate with you anymore.*

WHAT I NEED FROM YOU: *I need you to listen to more. If I say I need help, come help me. I need you to ask about my schedule and what's going on with me and the kids because sometimes I feel like a single parent. I need for us to discuss our schedules first with each other before we make plans for each other. I need you to speak to my love language through acts of service or gifts. If your work schedule is hectic and you're too tired to go to the store and purchase something, you can always order something for me and have it shipped to the house. Give me something to look forward to so I can know you're thinking of me and care about me.*

YOUR SPOUSE'S RESPONSE: *I realize that I have not been attentive to your needs and my work schedule has not allowed very much time for me to be home. Finances have really stressed me out at times where I feel the only solution is for me to work more hours. I do understand there needs to be some balance and your needs are important to me. I don't want you to feel neglected or overlooked. I also don't want to be inconsiderate or selfish with my time, so from now on I will be intentional about how I use my time and being mindful of your needs and your schedule. I don't like to work all the hours that I work and hope that one day I don't have to.*

PRAYER/SCRIPTURES TO BELIEVE GOD FOR: _God, I'm believing that my husband and I will grow in our marriage. I'm believing we will communicate better and that my husband will be more attentive to my needs and that I be more attentive to his. I'm believing we will not suffer from this issue any longer and this issue will be left in the past. God, I'm praying my husband understands me and helps out more with the kids. I'm believing God you can heal any hurt in our marriage that may be preventing us from hearing each other. Lord, I'm believing you to be my words that will impact change in my husband. I believe my husband will read this and want to help more and desire to grow in our marriage. I believe God you are doing something right now in my husband and I thank you in advance for it._

James 1:19, But let every man be swift to hear, slow to speak, slow to wrath.
Proverbs 16:24, Gracious words are like a honeycomb, sweetness to the soul & health to the body
Ephesians 4:29, Let no corrupting talk come out of your mouths, but only such as is good for building up, as fits the occasion, that it may give grace to those who hear.
Luke 18:27, But he said, What is impossible with man is possible with God.

DAILY DECLARATIONS: _I love my husband and he loves me._

My husband is willing to help and step in whenever I ask.

My husband is mindful of my needs and I am mindful of his needs

THE RESOLUTION:

- Plan ahead and put weekly/bi-weekly date nights on calendar

- Plan free or low budget dates that won't break the bank

- Be more understanding that my husband works very hard and needs time for rest

-Put on calendar the days my husband will help w/ housework, kids, cooking, etc.

SCRIPTURES CONCERNING:
FAMILY

———

PROVERBS 3:33 (NIV)
*The Lord's curse is on the house of the wicked,
but he blesses the home of the righteous..*

ISAIAH 54:13 (NIV)
*All your children will be taught by the Lord,
and great will be their peace.*

PSALM 102:28
*The children of your servants will live in your presence;
their descendants will be established before you.*

ISAIAH 41:13
*For I am the Lord your God who takes hold of your
right handand says to you, Do not fear; I will help you.*

ISAIAH 44:3B
*I will pour out my Spirit on your offspring,
and my blessing on your descendants.*

DEUTERONOMY 6:6-7
*These commandments that I give you today are to be on
your hearts. Impress them on your children. Talk about them
when you sit at home and when you walk along the road,
when you lie down and when you get up.*

PROVERB 22:6
*Start children off on the way they should go,
and even when they are old they will not turn from it.*

PSALM 127:3-5
*Children are a heritage from the Lord,offspring a reward
from him. Like arrows in the hands of a warrior
are children born in one's youth. Blessed is the man
whose quiver is full of them.They will not be put to shame
when they contend with their opponents in court.*

———

SCRIPTURES CONCERNING: *FORGIVENESS*

COLOSSIANS 3:13–14
Bear with each other and forgive one another if any of you has a grievance against someone. Forgive as the Lord forgave you. And over all these virtues put on love, which binds them all together in perfect unity.

EPHESIANS 4:31–32
Get rid of all bitterness, rage and anger, brawling and slander, along with every form of malice. Be kind and compassionate to one another, forgiving each other, just as in Christ God forgave you.

MATTHEW 6:14–15
For if you forgive other people when they sin against you, your heavenly Father will also forgive you. But if you do not forgive others their sins, your Father will not forgive your sins.

JOHN 20:23
If you forgive anyone's sins, their sins are forgiven; if you do not forgive them, they are not forgiven."

LUKE 6:36
Be merciful, just as your Father is merciful.

1 PETER 4:8
Above all, love each other deeply, because love covers over a multitude of sins.

1 CORINTHIANS 7:10
To the married I give this command (not I, but the Lord): A wife must not separate from her husband.

JAMES 5:16
Therefore confess your sins to each other and pray for each other so that you may be healed. The prayer of a righteous person is powerful and effective.

SCRIPTURES CONCERNING:
FINANCES

PROVERBS 3:9-10

Honor the Lord with your wealth,with the firstfruits of all your crops;then your barns will be filled to overflowing, and your vats will brim over with new wine.

JOHN 14:13

And I will do whatever you ask in my name, so that the Father may be glorified in the Son.

PHILLIPPIANS 4:19

And my God will meet all your needs according to the riches of his glory in Christ Jesus.

LUKE 6:38

Give, and it will be given to you. A good measure, pressed down, shaken together and running over, will be poured into your lap. For with the measure you use, it will be measured to you.

PSALM 20:4

May he give you the desire of your heart and make all your plans succeed.

2 CORINTHIANS 9:6-7

Remember this: Whoever sows sparingly will also reap sparingly, and whoever sows generously will also reap generously. Each of you should give what you have decided in your heart to give, not reluctantly or under compulsion, for God loves a cheerful giver.

MALACHI 3:10-11

Bring the whole tithe into the storehouse, that there may be food in my house. Test me in this," says the Lord Almighty, "and see if I will not throw open the floodgates of heaven and pour out so much blessing that there will not be room enough to store it. I will prevent pests from devouring your crops, and the vines in your fields will not drop their fruit before it is ripe," says the Lord Almighty.

SCRIPTURES CONCERNING: *INTIMACY*

1 CORINTHIANS 7:5

Do not deprive each other except perhaps by mutual consent and for a time, so that you may devote yourselves to prayer. Then come together again so that Satan will not tempt you because of your lack of self-control.

PROVERBS 18:22

He who finds a wife finds what is good and receives favor from the Lord.

GENESIS 2:23-24

The man said, "This is now bone of my bone and flesh of my flesh;she shall be called 'woman,'for she was taken out of man."That is why a man leaves his father and mother and is united to his wife, and they become one flesh.

SONG OF SONGS 7:8-10

I said, "I will climb the palm tree;I will take hold of its fruit."May your breasts be like clusters of grapes on the vine,the fragrance of your breath like apples, and your mouth like the best wine.

She: May the wine go straight to my beloved, flowing gently over lips and teeth. I belong to my beloved,and his desire is for me.

SONG OF SOLOMON 1:2

Let him kiss me with the kisses of his mouth: for thy love is better than wine.

RUTH 1:16

But Ruth replied, "Don't urge me to leave you or to turn back from you. Where you go I will go, and where you stay I will stay. Your people will be my people and your God my God.

SCRIPTURES CONCERNING:
COMMUNICATION

PROVERBS 15:1 (NKJV)
A soft answer turns away wrath, But a harsh word stirs up anger.

1 THESSALONIANS 5:11 (NKJV)
*So encourage each other to build each other up,
just as you are already doing.*

PHILIPPIANS 2:14-15
*Do everything without complaining and arguing, 15 so that
no one can criticize you. Live clean, innocent lives as
children of God, shining like bright lights in a world full of
crooked and perverse people.*

2 TIMOTHY 2:16
*Avoid worthless, foolish talk that only leads to more godless
behavior.*

PROVERBS 12:15
The way of fools seems right to them but the wise listen to advice.

EPHESIANS 4:15
*Instead, speaking the truth in love, we will grow to
become in every respect the mature body of him
who is the head, that is, Christ.*

PROVERBS 16:24
*Gracious words are a honeycomb,
sweet to the soul and healing to the bones.*

JAMES 1:19-22
*My dear brothers and sisters, take note of this: Everyone should
be quick to listen, slow to speak and slow to become angry,
because human anger does not produce the righteousness
that God desires. Therefore, get rid of all moral filth and the
evil that is so prevalent and humbly accept the word planted
in you, which can save you.*

*Do not merely listen to the word, and so deceive yourselves.
Do what it says.*

Communication
TO A RELATIONSHIP
IS LIKE OXYGEN
TO LIFE. WITHOUT IT
...IT DIES

TONY GASKINS

A Couple's Words

DATE: _____   TIME: _____

THE SITUATION: _____

_____
_____
_____
_____
_____
_____
_____
_____
_____
_____
_____
_____
_____
_____

WHAT I NEED FROM YOU: _____

_____
_____
_____
_____
_____
_____
_____
_____

YOUR SPOUSE'S RESPONSE: _____

_____
_____
_____
_____
_____
_____
_____
_____

PRAYER/SCRIPTURES TO BELIEVE GOD FOR:_____

_____
_____
_____
_____
_____
_____
_____
_____
_____
_____
_____
_____
_____
_____
_____

DAILY DECLARATIONS: _____

_____
_____
_____
_____
_____
_____
_____
_____
_____
_____
_____
_____

THE RESOLUTION: _____

_____
_____
_____
_____
_____
_____
_____

A Couple's Words

"Gracious words are like a honeycomb, sweetness to the soul and health to the body" (Proverbs 16:24)

DATE: _____ TIME: _____

THE SITUATION: _____
_____
_____
_____
_____
_____
_____
_____
_____
_____
_____
_____
_____
_____

WHAT I NEED FROM YOU: _____
_____
_____
_____
_____
_____
_____
_____
_____

YOUR SPOUSE'S RESPONSE: _____
_____
_____
_____
_____
_____
_____
_____

PRAYER/SCRIPTURES TO BELIEVE GOD FOR:_____

_____
_____
_____
_____
_____
_____
_____
_____
_____
_____
_____
_____
_____
_____
_____
_____

DAILY DECLARATIONS: _____

_____
_____
_____
_____
_____
_____
_____
_____
_____
_____
_____
_____
_____

THE RESOLUTION: _____

_____
_____
_____
_____
_____
_____
_____

A Couple's Words

DATE: _____ TIME: _____

THE SITUATION: _____
_____
_____
_____
_____
_____
_____
_____
_____
_____
_____
_____
_____

WHAT I NEED FROM YOU: _____
_____
_____
_____
_____
_____
_____
_____

YOUR SPOUSE'S RESPONSE: _____
_____
_____
_____
_____
_____
_____
_____

PRAYER/SCRIPTURES TO BELIEVE GOD FOR:_____

_____
_____
_____
_____
_____
_____
_____
_____
_____
_____
_____
_____
_____
_____
_____
_____
_____

DAILY DECLARATIONS: _____

_____
_____
_____
_____
_____
_____
_____
_____
_____
_____
_____
_____
_____

THE RESOLUTION: _____

_____
_____
_____
_____
_____
_____
_____

A Couple's Words

"Gracious words are like a honeycomb, sweetness to the soul and health to the body" (Proverbs 16:24)

DATE: _____ TIME: _____

THE SITUATION: _____
_____
_____
_____
_____
_____
_____
_____
_____
_____
_____
_____
_____
_____

WHAT I NEED FROM YOU: _____
_____
_____
_____
_____
_____
_____
_____

YOUR SPOUSE'S RESPONSE: _____
_____
_____
_____
_____
_____
_____
_____

PRAYER/SCRIPTURES TO BELIEVE GOD FOR:_____

_____
_____
_____
_____
_____
_____
_____
_____
_____
_____
_____
_____
_____
_____
_____
_____
_____

DAILY DECLARATIONS: _____

_____
_____
_____
_____
_____
_____
_____
_____
_____
_____
_____
_____
_____

THE RESOLUTION: _____

_____
_____
_____
_____
_____
_____
_____
_____

A Couple's Words

"Gracious words are like a honeycomb, sweetness to the soul and health to the body" (Proverbs 16:24)

DATE: _____ TIME: _____

THE SITUATION: _____

_____
_____
_____
_____
_____
_____
_____
_____
_____
_____
_____
_____
_____
_____

WHAT I NEED FROM YOU: _____

_____
_____
_____
_____
_____
_____
_____
_____

YOUR SPOUSE'S RESPONSE: _____

_____
_____
_____
_____
_____
_____
_____

PRAYER/SCRIPTURES TO BELIEVE GOD FOR:_____

_____
_____
_____
_____
_____
_____
_____
_____
_____
_____
_____
_____
_____
_____
_____
_____

DAILY DECLARATIONS: _____

_____
_____
_____
_____
_____
_____
_____
_____
_____
_____
_____
_____

THE RESOLUTION: _____

_____
_____
_____
_____
_____
_____
_____

A Couple's Words

"Gracious words are like a honeycomb, sweetness to the soul and health to the body" (Proverbs 16:24)

DATE: _____ TIME: _____

THE SITUATION: _____

_____
_____
_____
_____
_____
_____
_____
_____
_____
_____
_____
_____

WHAT I NEED FROM YOU: _____

_____
_____
_____
_____
_____
_____
_____

YOUR SPOUSE'S RESPONSE: _____

_____
_____
_____
_____
_____
_____
_____

PRAYER/SCRIPTURES TO BELIEVE GOD FOR:_____

_____
_____
_____
_____
_____
_____
_____
_____
_____
_____
_____
_____
_____
_____
_____

DAILY DECLARATIONS: _____

_____
_____
_____
_____
_____
_____
_____
_____
_____
_____
_____

THE RESOLUTION: _____

_____
_____
_____
_____
_____
_____
_____

A Couple's Words

"Gracious words are like a honeycomb, sweetness to the soul and health to the body" (Proverbs 16:24)

DATE: _____   TIME: _____

THE SITUATION: _____
_____
_____
_____
_____
_____
_____
_____
_____
_____
_____
_____
_____

WHAT I NEED FROM YOU: _____
_____
_____
_____
_____
_____
_____
_____

YOUR SPOUSE'S RESPONSE: _____
_____
_____
_____
_____
_____
_____

PRAYER/SCRIPTURES TO BELIEVE GOD FOR:_____

_____
_____
_____
_____
_____
_____
_____
_____
_____
_____
_____
_____
_____
_____
_____

DAILY DECLARATIONS: _____

_____
_____
_____
_____
_____
_____
_____
_____
_____
_____
_____
_____

THE RESOLUTION: _____

_____
_____
_____
_____
_____
_____
_____

A Couple's Words

"Gracious words are like a honeycomb, sweetness to the soul and health to the body" (Proverbs 16:24)

DATE: _____   TIME: _____

THE SITUATION: _____

_____
_____
_____
_____
_____
_____
_____
_____
_____
_____
_____
_____
_____
_____

WHAT I NEED FROM YOU: _____

_____
_____
_____
_____
_____
_____
_____
_____

YOUR SPOUSE'S RESPONSE: _____

_____
_____
_____
_____
_____
_____
_____

PRAYER/SCRIPTURES TO BELIEVE GOD FOR:_____

_____
_____
_____
_____
_____
_____
_____
_____
_____
_____
_____
_____
_____
_____
_____

DAILY DECLARATIONS: _____

_____
_____
_____
_____
_____
_____
_____
_____
_____
_____
_____
_____

THE RESOLUTION: _____

_____
_____
_____
_____
_____
_____
_____

A Couple's Words

"Gracious words are like a honeycomb, sweetness to the soul and health to the body" (Proverbs 16:24)

DATE: _____   TIME: _____

THE SITUATION: _____

_____
_____
_____
_____
_____
_____
_____
_____
_____
_____
_____
_____
_____
_____

WHAT I NEED FROM YOU: _____

_____
_____
_____
_____
_____
_____
_____
_____

YOUR SPOUSE'S RESPONSE: _____

_____
_____
_____
_____
_____
_____
_____

PRAYER/SCRIPTURES TO BELIEVE GOD FOR:_____

_____
_____
_____
_____
_____
_____
_____
_____
_____
_____
_____
_____
_____
_____
_____

DAILY DECLARATIONS: _____

_____
_____
_____
_____
_____
_____
_____
_____
_____
_____
_____
_____
_____

THE RESOLUTION: _____

_____
_____
_____
_____
_____
_____
_____

A Couple's Words

"Gracious words are like a honeycomb, sweetness to the soul and health to the body" (Proverbs 16:24)

DATE: _____   TIME: _____

THE SITUATION: _____
_____
_____
_____
_____
_____
_____
_____
_____
_____
_____
_____
_____
_____

WHAT I NEED FROM YOU: _____
_____
_____
_____
_____
_____
_____
_____

YOUR SPOUSE'S RESPONSE: _____
_____
_____
_____
_____
_____
_____
_____

PRAYER/SCRIPTURES TO BELIEVE GOD FOR:_____

_____
_____
_____
_____
_____
_____
_____
_____
_____
_____
_____
_____
_____
_____
_____

DAILY DECLARATIONS: _____

_____
_____
_____
_____
_____
_____
_____
_____
_____
_____
_____
_____

THE RESOLUTION: _____

_____
_____
_____
_____
_____
_____
_____

A Couple's Words

"Gracious words are like a honeycomb, sweetness to the soul and health to the body" (Proverbs 16:24)

DATE: _____   TIME: _____

THE SITUATION: _____
_____
_____
_____
_____
_____
_____
_____
_____
_____
_____
_____
_____
_____

WHAT I NEED FROM YOU: _____
_____
_____
_____
_____
_____
_____
_____
_____

YOUR SPOUSE'S RESPONSE: _____
_____
_____
_____
_____
_____
_____
_____

PRAYER/SCRIPTURES TO BELIEVE GOD FOR:_____

_____
_____
_____
_____
_____
_____
_____
_____
_____
_____
_____
_____
_____
_____
_____
_____

DAILY DECLARATIONS: _____

_____
_____
_____
_____
_____
_____
_____
_____
_____
_____
_____
_____

THE RESOLUTION: _____

_____
_____
_____
_____
_____
_____

A Couple's Words

"Gracious words are like a honeycomb, sweetness to the soul and health to the body" (Proverbs 16:24)

DATE: _____   TIME: _____

THE SITUATION: _____
_____
_____
_____
_____
_____
_____
_____
_____
_____
_____
_____
_____

WHAT I NEED FROM YOU: _____
_____
_____
_____
_____
_____
_____
_____

YOUR SPOUSE'S RESPONSE: _____
_____
_____
_____
_____
_____
_____
_____

PRAYER/SCRIPTURES TO BELIEVE GOD FOR:_____

_____
_____
_____
_____
_____
_____
_____
_____
_____
_____
_____
_____
_____
_____
_____
_____

DAILY DECLARATIONS: _____

_____
_____
_____
_____
_____
_____
_____
_____
_____
_____
_____
_____

THE RESOLUTION: _____

_____
_____
_____
_____
_____
_____
_____

A Couple's Words

"Gracious words are like a honeycomb, sweetness to the soul and health to the body" (Proverbs 16:24)

DATE: _____   TIME: _____

THE SITUATION: _____
_____
_____
_____
_____
_____
_____
_____
_____
_____
_____
_____
_____
_____

WHAT I NEED FROM YOU: _____
_____
_____
_____
_____
_____
_____
_____
_____

YOUR SPOUSE'S RESPONSE: _____
_____
_____
_____
_____
_____
_____
_____

PRAYER/SCRIPTURES TO BELIEVE GOD FOR:_____

_____
_____
_____
_____
_____
_____
_____
_____
_____
_____
_____
_____
_____
_____

DAILY DECLARATIONS: _____

_____
_____
_____
_____
_____
_____
_____
_____
_____
_____
_____

THE RESOLUTION: _____

_____
_____
_____
_____
_____
_____
_____

A Couple's Words

"Gracious words are like a honeycomb, sweetness to the soul and health to the body" (Proverbs 16:24)

DATE: _____ TIME: _____

THE SITUATION: _____

_____
_____
_____
_____
_____
_____
_____
_____
_____
_____
_____
_____
_____

WHAT I NEED FROM YOU: _____

_____
_____
_____
_____
_____
_____
_____
_____

YOUR SPOUSE'S RESPONSE: _____

_____
_____
_____
_____
_____
_____
_____

PRAYER/SCRIPTURES TO BELIEVE GOD FOR:_____

_____
_____
_____
_____
_____
_____
_____
_____
_____
_____
_____
_____
_____
_____
_____
_____

DAILY DECLARATIONS: _____

_____
_____
_____
_____
_____
_____
_____
_____
_____
_____
_____
_____
_____

THE RESOLUTION: _____

_____
_____
_____
_____
_____
_____
_____

A Couple's Words

"Gracious words are like a honeycomb, sweetness to the soul and health to the body" (Proverbs 16:24)

DATE: _____ TIME: _____

THE SITUATION: _____
_____
_____
_____
_____
_____
_____
_____
_____
_____
_____
_____
_____
_____
_____

WHAT I NEED FROM YOU: _____
_____
_____
_____
_____
_____
_____
_____
_____

YOUR SPOUSE'S RESPONSE: _____
_____
_____
_____
_____
_____
_____
_____

PRAYER/SCRIPTURES TO BELIEVE GOD FOR:_____

_____
_____
_____
_____
_____
_____
_____
_____
_____
_____
_____
_____
_____
_____
_____
_____

DAILY DECLARATIONS: _____

_____
_____
_____
_____
_____
_____
_____
_____
_____
_____
_____
_____
_____

THE RESOLUTION: _____

_____
_____
_____
_____
_____
_____
_____

A Couple's Words

"Gracious words are like a honeycomb, sweetness to the soul and health to the body" (Proverbs 16:24)

DATE: _____   TIME: _____

THE SITUATION: _____
_____
_____
_____
_____
_____
_____
_____
_____
_____
_____
_____
_____
_____

WHAT I NEED FROM YOU: _____
_____
_____
_____
_____
_____
_____
_____
_____

YOUR SPOUSE'S RESPONSE: _____
_____
_____
_____
_____
_____
_____
_____

PRAYER/SCRIPTURES TO BELIEVE GOD FOR:_____

_____
_____
_____
_____
_____
_____
_____
_____
_____
_____
_____
_____
_____
_____

DAILY DECLARATIONS: _____

_____
_____
_____
_____
_____
_____
_____
_____
_____
_____
_____

THE RESOLUTION: _____

_____
_____
_____
_____
_____
_____
_____

A Couple's Words

"Gracious words are like a honeycomb, sweetness to the soul and health to the body" (Proverbs 16:24)

DATE: _____   TIME: _____

THE SITUATION: _____

_____

_____

_____

_____

_____

_____

_____

_____

_____

_____

_____

_____

_____

WHAT I NEED FROM YOU: _____

_____

_____

_____

_____

_____

_____

_____

YOUR SPOUSE'S RESPONSE: _____

_____

_____

_____

_____

_____

_____

_____

PRAYER/SCRIPTURES TO BELIEVE GOD FOR:_____

_____
_____
_____
_____
_____
_____
_____
_____
_____
_____
_____
_____
_____
_____
_____
_____

DAILY DECLARATIONS: _____

_____
_____
_____
_____
_____
_____
_____
_____
_____
_____
_____
_____

THE RESOLUTION: _____

_____
_____
_____
_____
_____
_____
_____

A Couple's Words

"Gracious words are like a honeycomb, sweetness to the soul and health to the body" (Proverbs 16:24)

DATE: _____   TIME: _____

THE SITUATION: _____

_____
_____
_____
_____
_____
_____
_____
_____
_____
_____
_____
_____
_____
_____

WHAT I NEED FROM YOU: _____

_____
_____
_____
_____
_____
_____
_____
_____

YOUR SPOUSE'S RESPONSE: _____

_____
_____
_____
_____
_____
_____
_____

PRAYER/SCRIPTURES TO BELIEVE GOD FOR:_____

_____
_____
_____
_____
_____
_____
_____
_____
_____
_____
_____
_____
_____
_____
_____
_____

DAILY DECLARATIONS: _____

_____
_____
_____
_____
_____
_____
_____
_____
_____
_____
_____
_____

THE RESOLUTION: _____

_____
_____
_____
_____
_____
_____
_____

A Couple's Words

"Gracious words are like a honeycomb, sweetness to the soul and health to the body" (Proverbs 16:24)

DATE: _____   TIME: _____

THE SITUATION: _____
_____
_____
_____
_____
_____
_____
_____
_____
_____
_____
_____
_____

WHAT I NEED FROM YOU: _____
_____
_____
_____
_____
_____
_____
_____
_____

YOUR SPOUSE'S RESPONSE: _____
_____
_____
_____
_____
_____
_____
_____

PRAYER/SCRIPTURES TO BELIEVE GOD FOR:_____

_____
_____
_____
_____
_____
_____
_____
_____
_____
_____
_____
_____
_____
_____
_____

DAILY DECLARATIONS: _____

_____
_____
_____
_____
_____
_____
_____
_____
_____
_____
_____
_____

THE RESOLUTION: _____

_____
_____
_____
_____
_____
_____
_____

A Couple's Words

"Gracious words are like a honeycomb, sweetness to the soul and health to the body" (Proverbs 16:24)

DATE: _____   TIME: _____

THE SITUATION: _____

_____
_____
_____
_____
_____
_____
_____
_____
_____
_____
_____
_____
_____

WHAT I NEED FROM YOU: _____

_____
_____
_____
_____
_____
_____
_____
_____

YOUR SPOUSE'S RESPONSE: _____

_____
_____
_____
_____
_____
_____
_____

PRAYER/SCRIPTURES TO BELIEVE GOD FOR:_____

_____
_____
_____
_____
_____
_____
_____
_____
_____
_____
_____
_____
_____
_____
_____

DAILY DECLARATIONS: _____

_____
_____
_____
_____
_____
_____
_____
_____
_____
_____
_____
_____

THE RESOLUTION: _____

_____
_____
_____
_____
_____
_____
_____

A Couple's Words

"Gracious words are like a honeycomb, sweetness to the soul and health to the body" (Proverbs 16:24)

DATE: _____ TIME: _____

THE SITUATION: _____
_____
_____
_____
_____
_____
_____
_____
_____
_____
_____
_____
_____
_____

WHAT I NEED FROM YOU: _____
_____
_____
_____
_____
_____
_____
_____
_____

YOUR SPOUSE'S RESPONSE: _____
_____
_____
_____
_____
_____
_____
_____

PRAYER/SCRIPTURES TO BELIEVE GOD FOR:_____

_____
_____
_____
_____
_____
_____
_____
_____
_____
_____
_____
_____
_____
_____
_____
_____

DAILY DECLARATIONS: _____

_____
_____
_____
_____
_____
_____
_____
_____
_____
_____
_____
_____
_____

THE RESOLUTION: _____

_____
_____
_____
_____
_____
_____
_____

A Couple's Words

"Gracious words are like a honeycomb, sweetness to the soul and health to the body" (Proverbs 16:24)

DATE: _____ TIME: _____

THE SITUATION: _____

_____
_____
_____
_____
_____
_____
_____
_____
_____
_____
_____
_____
_____
_____

WHAT I NEED FROM YOU: _____

_____
_____
_____
_____
_____
_____
_____
_____

YOUR SPOUSE'S RESPONSE: _____

_____
_____
_____
_____
_____
_____
_____
_____

PRAYER/SCRIPTURES TO BELIEVE GOD FOR: _____

_____
_____
_____
_____
_____
_____
_____
_____
_____
_____
_____
_____
_____
_____
_____
_____

DAILY DECLARATIONS: _____

_____
_____
_____
_____
_____
_____
_____
_____
_____
_____
_____
_____

THE RESOLUTION: _____

_____
_____
_____
_____
_____
_____
_____

A Couple's Words

"Gracious words are like a honeycomb, sweetness to the soul and health to the body" (Proverbs 16:24)

DATE: _____   TIME: _____

THE SITUATION: _____
_____
_____
_____
_____
_____
_____
_____
_____
_____
_____
_____
_____
_____

WHAT I NEED FROM YOU: _____
_____
_____
_____
_____
_____
_____
_____

YOUR SPOUSE'S RESPONSE: _____
_____
_____
_____
_____
_____
_____

PRAYER/SCRIPTURES TO BELIEVE GOD FOR:_____

_____
_____
_____
_____
_____
_____
_____
_____
_____
_____
_____
_____
_____
_____
_____
_____

DAILY DECLARATIONS: _____

_____
_____
_____
_____
_____
_____
_____
_____
_____
_____
_____
_____

THE RESOLUTION: _____

_____
_____
_____
_____
_____
_____
_____

A Couple's Words

"Gracious words are like a honeycomb, sweetness to the soul and health to the body" (Proverbs 16:24)

DATE: _____   TIME: _____

THE SITUATION: _____
_____
_____
_____
_____
_____
_____
_____
_____
_____
_____
_____
_____
_____

WHAT I NEED FROM YOU: _____
_____
_____
_____
_____
_____
_____
_____
_____

YOUR SPOUSE'S RESPONSE: _____
_____
_____
_____
_____
_____
_____
_____

PRAYER/SCRIPTURES TO BELIEVE GOD FOR:_____

_____
_____
_____
_____
_____
_____
_____
_____
_____
_____
_____
_____
_____
_____
_____
_____

DAILY DECLARATIONS: _____

_____
_____
_____
_____
_____
_____
_____
_____
_____
_____
_____
_____
_____

THE RESOLUTION: _____

_____
_____
_____
_____
_____
_____
_____

A Couple's Words

"Gracious words are like a honeycomb, sweetness to the soul and health to the body" (Proverbs 16:24)

DATE: _____   TIME: _____

THE SITUATION: _____

_____
_____
_____
_____
_____
_____
_____
_____
_____
_____
_____
_____
_____

WHAT I NEED FROM YOU: _____

_____
_____
_____
_____
_____
_____
_____
_____

YOUR SPOUSE'S RESPONSE: _____

_____
_____
_____
_____
_____
_____
_____

PRAYER/SCRIPTURES TO BELIEVE GOD FOR:_____

_____
_____
_____
_____
_____
_____
_____
_____
_____
_____
_____
_____
_____
_____
_____

DAILY DECLARATIONS: _____

_____
_____
_____
_____
_____
_____
_____
_____
_____
_____
_____
_____

THE RESOLUTION: _____

_____
_____
_____
_____
_____
_____
_____

A Couple's Words

"Gracious words are like a honeycomb, sweetness to the soul and health to the body" (Proverbs 16:24)

DATE: _____   TIME: _____

THE SITUATION: _____

_____
_____
_____
_____
_____
_____
_____
_____
_____
_____
_____
_____
_____
_____

WHAT I NEED FROM YOU: _____

_____
_____
_____
_____
_____
_____
_____
_____

YOUR SPOUSE'S RESPONSE: _____

_____
_____
_____
_____
_____
_____
_____

PRAYER/SCRIPTURES TO BELIEVE GOD FOR:_____

_____
_____
_____
_____
_____
_____
_____
_____
_____
_____
_____
_____
_____
_____
_____
_____
_____

DAILY DECLARATIONS: _____

_____
_____
_____
_____
_____
_____
_____
_____
_____
_____
_____
_____
_____

THE RESOLUTION: _____

_____
_____
_____
_____
_____
_____
_____

A Couple's Words

"Gracious words are like a honeycomb, sweetness to the soul and health to the body" (Proverbs 16:24)

DATE: _____ TIME: _____

THE SITUATION: _____

_____
_____
_____
_____
_____
_____
_____
_____
_____
_____
_____
_____

WHAT I NEED FROM YOU: _____

_____
_____
_____
_____
_____
_____
_____

YOUR SPOUSE'S RESPONSE: _____

_____
_____
_____
_____
_____
_____

PRAYER/SCRIPTURES TO BELIEVE GOD FOR:_____

_____
_____
_____
_____
_____
_____
_____
_____
_____
_____
_____
_____
_____
_____
_____
_____

DAILY DECLARATIONS: _____

_____
_____
_____
_____
_____
_____
_____
_____
_____
_____
_____
_____

THE RESOLUTION: _____

_____
_____
_____
_____
_____
_____
_____

A Couple's Words

"Gracious words are like a honeycomb, sweetness to the soul and health to the body" (Proverbs 16:24)

DATE: _____ TIME: _____

THE SITUATION: _____
_____
_____
_____
_____
_____
_____
_____
_____
_____
_____
_____
_____

WHAT I NEED FROM YOU: _____
_____
_____
_____
_____
_____
_____
_____

YOUR SPOUSE'S RESPONSE: _____
_____
_____
_____
_____
_____
_____
_____

PRAYER/SCRIPTURES TO BELIEVE GOD FOR:_____

_____
_____
_____
_____
_____
_____
_____
_____
_____
_____
_____
_____
_____
_____
_____
_____
_____

DAILY DECLARATIONS: _____

_____
_____
_____
_____
_____
_____
_____
_____
_____
_____
_____
_____
_____

THE RESOLUTION: _____

_____
_____
_____
_____
_____
_____
_____

A Couple's Words

"Gracious words are like a honeycomb, sweetness to the soul and health to the body" (Proverbs 16:24)

DATE: _____   TIME: _____

THE SITUATION: _____

_____
_____
_____
_____
_____
_____
_____
_____
_____
_____
_____
_____
_____

WHAT I NEED FROM YOU:

_____
_____
_____
_____
_____
_____
_____
_____

YOUR SPOUSE'S RESPONSE: _____

_____
_____
_____
_____
_____
_____
_____

PRAYER/SCRIPTURES TO BELIEVE GOD FOR:_____

_____
_____
_____
_____
_____
_____
_____
_____
_____
_____
_____
_____
_____
_____
_____
_____

DAILY DECLARATIONS: _____

_____
_____
_____
_____
_____
_____
_____
_____
_____
_____
_____
_____
_____

THE RESOLUTION: _____

_____
_____
_____
_____
_____
_____
_____

A Couple's Words

"Gracious words are like a honeycomb, sweetness to the soul and health to the body" (Proverbs 16:24)

DATE: _____   TIME: _____

THE SITUATION: _____

_____
_____
_____
_____
_____
_____
_____
_____
_____
_____
_____
_____
_____
_____

WHAT I NEED FROM YOU:

_____
_____
_____
_____
_____
_____
_____
_____
_____

YOUR SPOUSE'S RESPONSE: _____

_____
_____
_____
_____
_____
_____
_____

PRAYER/SCRIPTURES TO BELIEVE GOD FOR:_____

_____
_____
_____
_____
_____
_____
_____
_____
_____
_____
_____
_____
_____
_____
_____
_____

DAILY DECLARATIONS: _____

_____
_____
_____
_____
_____
_____
_____
_____
_____
_____
_____
_____

THE RESOLUTION: _____

_____
_____
_____
_____
_____
_____
_____

A Couple's Words

"Gracious words are like a honeycomb, sweetness to the soul and health to the body" (Proverbs 16:24)

DATE: _____   TIME: _____

THE SITUATION: _____

_____
_____
_____
_____
_____
_____
_____
_____
_____
_____
_____
_____
_____
_____

WHAT I NEED FROM YOU: _____

_____
_____
_____
_____
_____
_____
_____
_____

YOUR SPOUSE'S RESPONSE: _____

_____
_____
_____
_____
_____
_____
_____

PRAYER/SCRIPTURES TO BELIEVE GOD FOR:_____

_____
_____
_____
_____
_____
_____
_____
_____
_____
_____
_____
_____
_____
_____
_____
_____
_____

DAILY DECLARATIONS: _____

_____
_____
_____
_____
_____
_____
_____
_____
_____
_____
_____
_____
_____

THE RESOLUTION: _____

_____
_____
_____
_____
_____
_____
_____

A Couple's Words

"Gracious words are like a honeycomb, sweetness to the soul and health to the body" (Proverbs 16:24)

DATE: _____   TIME: _____

THE SITUATION: _____
_____
_____
_____
_____
_____
_____
_____
_____
_____
_____
_____
_____
_____

WHAT I NEED FROM YOU: _____
_____
_____
_____
_____
_____
_____
_____
_____

YOUR SPOUSE'S RESPONSE: _____
_____
_____
_____
_____
_____
_____
_____

PRAYER/SCRIPTURES TO BELIEVE GOD FOR:_____

_____
_____
_____
_____
_____
_____
_____
_____
_____
_____
_____
_____
_____
_____
_____
_____

DAILY DECLARATIONS: _____

_____
_____
_____
_____
_____
_____
_____
_____
_____
_____
_____
_____

THE RESOLUTION: _____

_____
_____
_____
_____
_____
_____

A Couple's Words

"Gracious words are like a honeycomb, sweetness to the soul and health to the body" (Proverbs 16:24)

DATE: _____ TIME: _____

THE SITUATION: _____
_____
_____
_____
_____
_____
_____
_____
_____
_____
_____
_____
_____
_____
_____

WHAT I NEED FROM YOU: _____
_____
_____
_____
_____
_____
_____
_____
_____

YOUR SPOUSE'S RESPONSE: _____
_____
_____
_____
_____
_____
_____
_____

PRAYER/SCRIPTURES TO BELIEVE GOD FOR:_____

_____
_____
_____
_____
_____
_____
_____
_____
_____
_____
_____
_____
_____
_____
_____
_____
_____

DAILY DECLARATIONS: _____

_____
_____
_____
_____
_____
_____
_____
_____
_____
_____
_____
_____
_____

THE RESOLUTION: _____

_____
_____
_____
_____
_____
_____
_____

A Couple's Words

"Gracious words are like a honeycomb, sweetness to the soul and health to the body" (Proverbs 16:24)

DATE: _____   TIME: _____

THE SITUATION: _____

_____
_____
_____
_____
_____
_____
_____
_____
_____
_____
_____
_____
_____

WHAT I NEED FROM YOU: _____

_____
_____
_____
_____
_____
_____
_____
_____

YOUR SPOUSE'S RESPONSE: _____

_____
_____
_____
_____
_____
_____
_____

PRAYER/SCRIPTURES TO BELIEVE GOD FOR:_____

_____
_____
_____
_____
_____
_____
_____
_____
_____
_____
_____
_____
_____
_____
_____
_____
_____

DAILY DECLARATIONS: _____

_____
_____
_____
_____
_____
_____
_____
_____
_____
_____
_____
_____
_____

THE RESOLUTION: _____

_____
_____
_____
_____
_____
_____
_____

A Couple's Words

"Gracious words are like a honeycomb, sweetness to the soul and health to the body" (Proverbs 16:24)

DATE: _____   TIME: _____

THE SITUATION: _____
_____
_____
_____
_____
_____
_____
_____
_____
_____
_____
_____
_____
_____

WHAT I NEED FROM YOU: _____
_____
_____
_____
_____
_____
_____
_____

YOUR SPOUSE'S RESPONSE: _____
_____
_____
_____
_____
_____
_____
_____

PRAYER/SCRIPTURES TO BELIEVE GOD FOR:_____

_____
_____
_____
_____
_____
_____
_____
_____
_____
_____
_____
_____
_____
_____

DAILY DECLARATIONS: _____

_____
_____
_____
_____
_____
_____
_____
_____
_____
_____
_____
_____

THE RESOLUTION: _____

_____
_____
_____
_____
_____
_____
_____

A Couple's Words

"Gracious words are like a honeycomb, sweetness to the soul and health to the body" (Proverbs 16:24)

DATE: _____ TIME: _____

THE SITUATION: _____
_____
_____
_____
_____
_____
_____
_____
_____
_____
_____
_____
_____
_____

WHAT I NEED FROM YOU: _____
_____
_____
_____
_____
_____
_____
_____
_____

YOUR SPOUSE'S RESPONSE: _____
_____
_____
_____
_____
_____
_____
_____

PRAYER/SCRIPTURES TO BELIEVE GOD FOR:_____

_____
_____
_____
_____
_____
_____
_____
_____
_____
_____
_____
_____
_____
_____
_____
_____

DAILY DECLARATIONS: _____

_____
_____
_____
_____
_____
_____
_____
_____
_____
_____
_____
_____
_____

THE RESOLUTION: _____

_____
_____
_____
_____
_____
_____
_____

A Couple's Words

"Gracious words are like a honeycomb, sweetness to the soul and health to the body" (Proverbs 16:24)

DATE: _____   TIME: _____

THE SITUATION: _____

_____
_____
_____
_____
_____
_____
_____
_____
_____
_____
_____
_____
_____

WHAT I NEED FROM YOU: _____

_____
_____
_____
_____
_____
_____
_____

YOUR SPOUSE'S RESPONSE: _____

_____
_____
_____
_____
_____
_____

PRAYER/SCRIPTURES TO BELIEVE GOD FOR:_____

_____
_____
_____
_____
_____
_____
_____
_____
_____
_____
_____
_____
_____
_____
_____
_____

DAILY DECLARATIONS: _____

_____
_____
_____
_____
_____
_____
_____
_____
_____
_____
_____
_____
_____

THE RESOLUTION: _____

_____
_____
_____
_____
_____
_____
_____

A Couple's Words

"Gracious words are like a honeycomb, sweetness to the soul and health to the body" (Proverbs 16:24)

DATE: _____   TIME: _____

THE SITUATION: _____
_____
_____
_____
_____
_____
_____
_____
_____
_____
_____
_____
_____
_____

WHAT I NEED FROM YOU: _____
_____
_____
_____
_____
_____
_____
_____

YOUR SPOUSE'S RESPONSE: _____
_____
_____
_____
_____
_____
_____

PRAYER/SCRIPTURES TO BELIEVE GOD FOR:_____

_____
_____
_____
_____
_____
_____
_____
_____
_____
_____
_____
_____
_____
_____
_____

DAILY DECLARATIONS: _____

_____
_____
_____
_____
_____
_____
_____
_____
_____
_____
_____
_____

THE RESOLUTION: _____

_____
_____
_____
_____
_____
_____
_____

A Couple's Words

"Gracious words are like a honeycomb, sweetness to the soul and health to the body" (Proverbs 16:24)

DATE: _____   TIME: _____

THE SITUATION: _____

_____
_____
_____
_____
_____
_____
_____
_____
_____
_____
_____
_____
_____
_____

WHAT I NEED FROM YOU: _____

_____
_____
_____
_____
_____
_____
_____
_____
_____

YOUR SPOUSE'S RESPONSE: _____

_____
_____
_____
_____
_____
_____
_____

PRAYER/SCRIPTURES TO BELIEVE GOD FOR:_____

_____
_____
_____
_____
_____
_____
_____
_____
_____
_____
_____
_____
_____
_____
_____
_____

DAILY DECLARATIONS: _____

_____
_____
_____
_____
_____
_____
_____
_____
_____
_____
_____
_____
_____

THE RESOLUTION: _____

_____
_____
_____
_____
_____
_____
_____

A Couple's Words

"Gracious words are like a honeycomb, sweetness to the soul and health to the body" (Proverbs 16:24)

DATE: _____   TIME: _____

THE SITUATION: _____

_____
_____
_____
_____
_____
_____
_____
_____
_____
_____
_____
_____
_____
_____

WHAT I NEED FROM YOU: _____

_____
_____
_____
_____
_____
_____
_____
_____
_____

YOUR SPOUSE'S RESPONSE: _____

_____
_____
_____
_____
_____
_____
_____
_____

PRAYER/SCRIPTURES TO BELIEVE GOD FOR:_____

_____
_____
_____
_____
_____
_____
_____
_____
_____
_____
_____
_____
_____
_____
_____
_____
_____

DAILY DECLARATIONS: _____

_____
_____
_____
_____
_____
_____
_____
_____
_____
_____
_____
_____
_____

THE RESOLUTION: _____

_____
_____
_____
_____
_____
_____
_____

A Couple's Words

"Gracious words are like a honeycomb, sweetness to the soul and health to the body" (Proverbs 16:24)

DATE: _____   TIME: _____

THE SITUATION: _____

_____
_____
_____
_____
_____
_____
_____
_____
_____
_____
_____
_____
_____

WHAT I NEED FROM YOU:

_____
_____
_____
_____
_____
_____
_____
_____

YOUR SPOUSE'S RESPONSE: _____

_____
_____
_____
_____
_____
_____
_____

PRAYER/SCRIPTURES TO BELIEVE GOD FOR:_____

_____
_____
_____
_____
_____
_____
_____
_____
_____
_____
_____
_____
_____
_____
_____
_____
_____

DAILY DECLARATIONS: _____

_____
_____
_____
_____
_____
_____
_____
_____
_____
_____
_____
_____
_____

THE RESOLUTION: _____

_____
_____
_____
_____
_____
_____

❤ Couple's Bucket List ❤

TOGETHER LET'S...

♡ Read the same book	♡ Kiss in the rain
♡ Go skinny dipping	♡ Spend all day cuddling
♡ Volunteer together	♡ Take a road trip
♡	♡
♡	♡
♡	♡
♡	♡
♡	♡
♡	♡
♡	♡
♡	♡
♡	♡
♡	♡
♡	♡